INSTANT
MATH GA[MES]
THAT TEAC[H]

38 Hands-On Math Games

Written by Adela Garcia

Edited by Patricia Sarka

Illustrated by Patty Briles

Project Director Sue Lewis

Table of Contents

Introduction

How to Use This Book 4

Ideas for Using *Instant Math Games That Teach* 5

Individual Games

Leapfrog 10

100-Yard Dash 12

Tangram Teasers 14

Changing Places 16

Finding 50 18

Switch 20

Mazition (Maze Addition) 22

Pentominoes 24

Pick 6 26

Freedom 28

Hide and Seek 30

Mixed-up Music 32

Detour 34

Neighbors 36

Planet Puzzler 38

Martian Math 40

Magic 18 42

Mysterious Wonder Wheel 44

Games for Two

Snap 48

Kaboom! 50

Triple Play 52

Sink or Swim 54

Lightning 56

Three-in-a-Row 58
Add It Up 60
Cover Up (Greater, Less, Equal) 62
Exact Change 64
Pentomino Challenge 66
Round Up 68
Tic Tac 15 70
Ah-ha • Power • Nada 72

Games for Two or More

Snail's Pace 76
Spill the Beans 78
Blank Check 80
Continent Hop 82
Cross the River 84
Black Hole 86
Monster Math 88

Appendix and Game Answers

Markers 92
Number Circles 93
Number Squares & Tiles 94
Spinners 95
Dice 97
Tangram Pieces 99
Pentominoes 100
Math Wallet 101
Math Trophy 102
Game Answers 103

Instant Math Games That Teach

Instant Math Games That Teach provides teachers and students with 38 fun-filled, skill-packed math games. Each game includes a gameboard with simple, step-by-step instructions. These games target and reinforce specific math strategies and are intended to stimulate, challenge and excite young minds. They offer a wide variety of classroom uses, are adaptable to varying instructional objectives and may be used to supplement, enhance and enrich any math program.

Each *Instant Math Game* includes:

- An exciting *Instant Math* gameboard
- Easy-to-follow game rules
- Specific skills reinforced by the game
- Materials needed to play the game
- Objective of the game
- Number of players needed

How to Use This Book

The games in this book will provide your students with hours of fun and stimulating math reinforcement. For your convenience, this book is divided into three game sections (individual games, games for two, games for two or more) and an appendix. Easier games are at the beginning of each section. We suggest that for durability and flexibility of play, each gameboard and its directions be reproduced on sturdy paper and laminated before use by students.

INDIVIDUAL GAMES
Challenge individual students with these fast-paced games. With slight changes, many of these games can be converted into multi-player activities.

GAMES FOR TWO
These are games designed to be played by two players. Encourage students to alternate "going first" as the first player often has the advantage in these activities.

GAMES FOR TWO OR MORE
These games are for multiple players. Some work well as large group activities and can be used when you want the entire class to participate.

APPENDIX
Essential game pieces (not included on the gameboard) can be found in the Appendix. Check the Materials Needed section on the direction page for a complete list of materials. Math Fair awards and a handy Math Wallet for game piece storage are also included in the Appendix.

Ideas for Using *Instant Math Games That Teach*

CLASS ACTIVITIES

- Reproduce multiple copies of the same gameboard so everyone can participate in the same game.
- Copy the gameboard onto a transparency and use with an overhead projector.
- Designate one day a week as Math Game Day.

SMALL GROUP ACTIVITIES

- Use games to reinforce a specific math skill for students who need the extra practice.

INDIVIDUAL ACTIVITIES

- Encourage students to use games as a free-time activity when they have finished classwork.
- Make games available as "filler" activities—during attendance count, before recess, after an assembly.
- Some games take more than one sitting to solve. Allow students to keep harder-to-solve games at their desks so they can work on them in their spare time.

LEARNING CENTERS

Learning Centers are a great way to get *Instant Math Games* into the hands of all your students. Organize your *Instant Math Games* by placing individual games in file folders or large envelopes and keeping them in a designated area.

File Folder Games

Reproduce the gameboard and direction page on paper. Glue both sheets inside a file folder and laminate for added durability. Put game pieces in Math Wallet or a resealable plastic bag and paper clip or staple to file folder. Write the name of the game on the folder tab. Include a record sheet for students to keep track of games completed.

Envelope Games

Reproduce gameboard and direction page on sturdy paper. Laminate for added durability. Place inside large manila envelope along with any game pieces. On the outside of the envelope write the name of the game, the skills reinforced by the game and the number of players needed to play the game.

HOMEWORK
- Assign games as homework when skills need reinforcement. Games can be played alone or with a family member.
- As an extension activity, the student and family can design an original game to share with classmates.

MATH BUDDIES
Make arrangements with fellow teachers (in lower or higher grades) to pair students from both classes as Math Buddies. Once a week, for approximately 20 minutes, have Math Buddies play *Instant Math Games* together. Don't limit play to only those games designated for two or more players. Older students can monitor younger students' progress on individual games.

MATH FAIR
- Plan a Math Fair using these *Instant Math Games* and any original student-made games they inspired.
- Use the trophy pattern in the appendix to make Math Fair awards.

MARKERS
Most of the INSTANT MATH GAMES require players to use markers. Although generic paper markers are included in the appendix of this book, students will enjoy using a wide variety of markers. Start collecting now. Include students in the collection process.

Here are a few ideas:
- colorful plastic "poker" chips
- markers from commercial games
- coins—pennies, nickels, foreign coins
- small wooden/plastic blocks, Unifix cubes
- dry beans
- pasta
- buttons
- nuts and bolts
- paper clips/brass fasteners
- colorful stickers

OPTIONAL GAME MATERIALS

The following items are suggested for several *Instant Math Games.*
Collect and place in a box labeled Instant Math Game Materials.

- egg timer
- clock with second hand
- beans and macaroni to be used as counters
- empty 35mm film canisters for storing markers and counters
- snack-size plastic bags for storing game pieces
- an assortment of plastic dice
- small calculator
- box of scratch paper and pencils

GAMES FOR THE YOUNGER CHILD

The games at the beginning of each section are the easier games.
Choose those games that are appropriate to the ability of your
individual students. Different students will be able to play different
games. Some of the more challenging games will provide excellent
enrichment for the more capable students in your class.

Before asking younger students to play these games on their own, it is
important that you play them with the entire class or in small groups.
There are several ways to do this.

- Play the game using the overhead projector.
- Play the game on the chalkboard.
- Give each child a copy of the game and play as a whole class.
- Teach a few students the game and have them teach the other students.

GOING BEYOND

Challenge your students by asking them to share their strategies for
solving the games, either verbally or in written form. Students can
compare their strategies at the designated Learning Center or during
a group discussion.

Ask students to change or improve upon the games. Have them share
their changes. Also, encourage students to create their own games using
math concepts you are covering in class.

Individual Games

LEAPFROG

Skill
Problem solving

Materials Needed
- *Leapfrog* gameboard
- 14 markers (coins, game chips, buttons)

Object of Game
To remove all markers except one

Number of Players
One

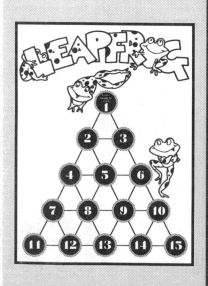

How to Play

1. Place one marker on every circle, except for circle #1. Leave it empty.

2. The game is played by jumping one marker at a time over another marker, landing in an empty circle. When a marker is jumped, it is removed from the gameboard.

> **Important:** Play begins by moving the marker in circle #4 to circle #1 and removing the marker in circle #2. Or it can be done by moving the marker in circle #6 to circle #1 and removing the marker in circle #3.

3. You can only jump adjacent markers (ones that are attached by a line).

4. Continue jumping over and removing markers until you have no other jumps to make. How many markers are left on the gameboard?

5. The ultimate goal of the game is to remove all markers except one. You may not succeed right away, but keep playing. You'll probably remove more markers with each game.

100-YARD DASH

Skill
Addition or multiplication facts

Materials Needed
- *100-Yard Dash* gameboard
- Pencil with eraser
- Stopwatch or clock with a second hand

Object of Game
To complete the track as quickly as possible by computing all the math facts around the course

Number of Players
One

How to Play

1. Select a number from 1 to 10.

2. Decide whether you will add or multiply the numbers around the track.

3. Write the operation and the number in the middle of the track.

4. Find the Starting Line.

5. Start timing yourself. Write the operation (+ or x) and the number in the square under the 7. Fill in the answer. Then move left and do the same with the rest of the numbers.

6. When you reach the Finish Line, note your time and record it on a separate sheet of paper.

7. Check your work and record how many of your answers are correct.

8. Repeat steps 1 through 6. Try to beat your time and accuracy records.

Teacher Tip
Laminate this gameboard and use with dry-erase pens or crayons or reproduce multiple copies for each player.

Instant Math Games That Teach

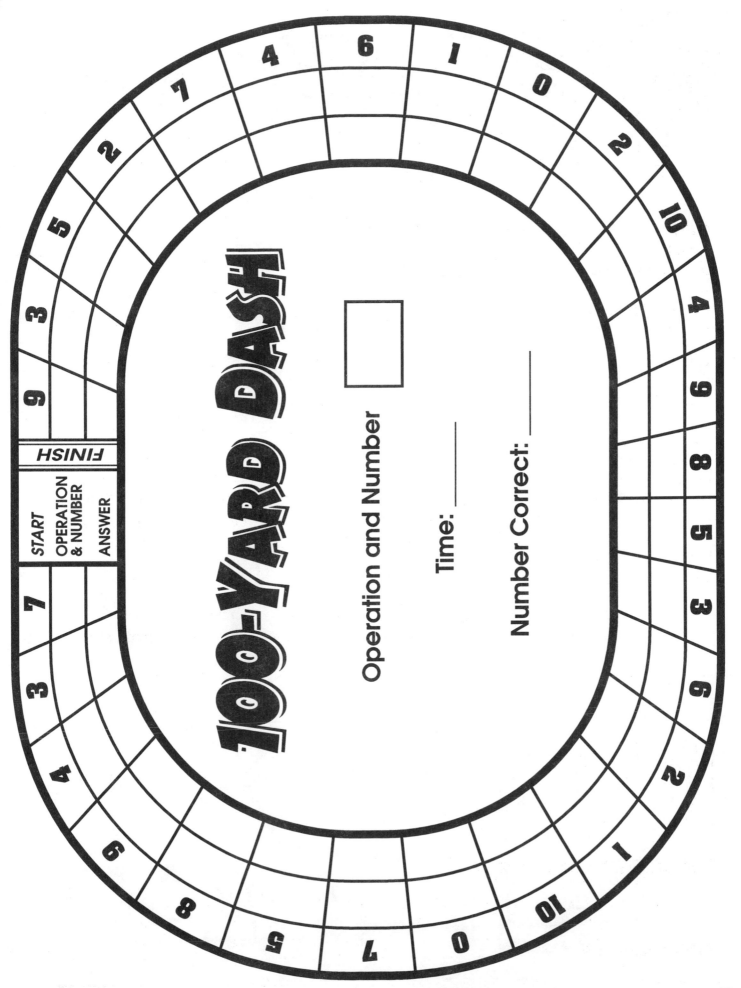

100-YARD DASH!

Operation and Number

Time: _____

Number Correct: _____

START	FINISH
OPERATION & NUMBER	
ANSWER	

TANGRAM TEASERS

Skill
Spatial relationships, problem solving

Materials Needed
- *Tangram Teasers* gameboard
- 7 tangram pieces (page 99)

Object of Game
To reproduce designs with tangram pieces

Number of Players
One

How to Play

1. Choose one of the tangram designs on the gameboard.

2. Using the tangram pieces, try to reproduce the design.

3. Once you've completed a design, mix up the tangram pieces and choose another design to reproduce. How many can you do?

4. Now make your own designs. Ask your classmates to reproduce them with their own tangrams.

TANGRAM TEASERS

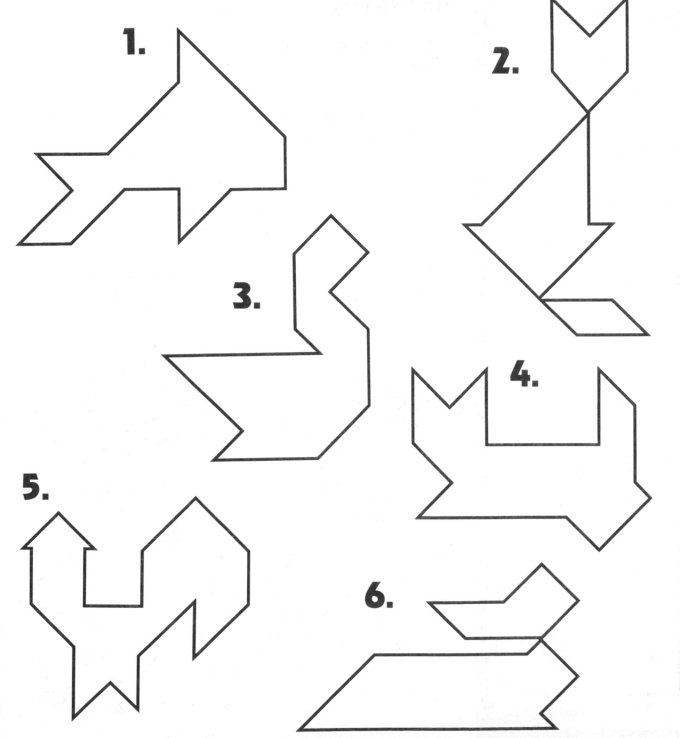

1.

2.

3.

4.

5.

6.

CHANGING PLACES

Skills
Spatial relationships, problem solving

Materials Needed
- *Changing Places* gameboard
- 9 markers (beans, coins, plastic chips)

Object of Game
To move only two markers in order to have two lines of five markers

Number of Players
One

How to Play

1. Place one marker in each of the circles on the gameboard.

2. Move only two markers so that you have two lines of five markers each.

3. How many moves did it take you? You should be able to complete this puzzle in only two moves!

On Your Own
Create your own Changing Places puzzle. Have a classmate play your game.

CHANGING PLACES

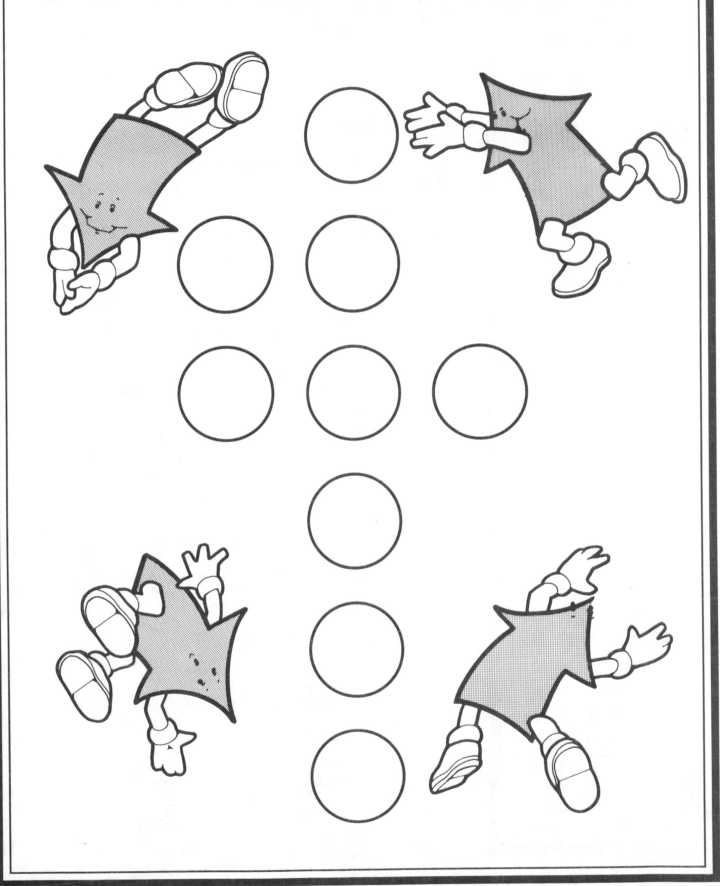

FINDING 50

Skills

Addition, using a calculator, practicing mental math, writing equations, estimation

Materials Needed

- *Finding 50* gameboard
- Scratch paper and pencil
- Calculator (optional)

Object of Game

To find three squares that touch and, when added together, equal 50

Number of Players

One

How to Play

1. Using mental math, scratch paper or a calculator, find three squares that touch at some horizontal, vertical or diagonal point and add up to 50.

2. When you find the three numbers, write them as an equation.

For example, $26 + 14 + 10 = 50$.

Be on the lookout!
There is more than one set of numbers that add up to 50. Be on the lookout for all the combinations.

FINDING 50

12	30	9	17	31	16
7	3	6	21	23	32
2	19	11	8	14	10
13	20	25	28	17	9
26	16	4	18	10	30
11	5	27	9	29	33

FINDING 50

12	30	9	17	31	16
7	3	6	21	23	32
2	19	11	8	14	10
13	20	25	28	17	9
26	16	4	18	10	30
11	5	27	9	29	33

SWITCH

Skill
Strategy

Materials Needed
- *Switch* gameboard
- 2 sets of 2 markers (for example, 2 pennies and 2 nickels or 2 red plastic chips and 2 blue plastic chips)

Object of Game
To exchange markers in as few moves as possible

Number of Players
One

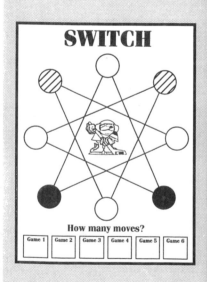

How to Play

1. Place two of the same kind of marker on the striped circles.

2. Place the other two markers on the black circles.

3. Move one marker at a time along a line, from circle to circle. (No two markers can be in one circle at the same time.)

4. Count your moves.

5. Keep moving markers, one at a time, until all markers have exchanged places. (Markers beginning on the striped circles must end up on the black circles; markers beginning on the black circles must end up on the striped circles.)

6. Record the number of moves on a scoresheet. The object is to use as few moves as possible.

7. Repeat the game (steps 1–5), trying to beat your record.

Teacher Tip
Make multiple copies so that each student has his/her own gameboard.

SWITCH

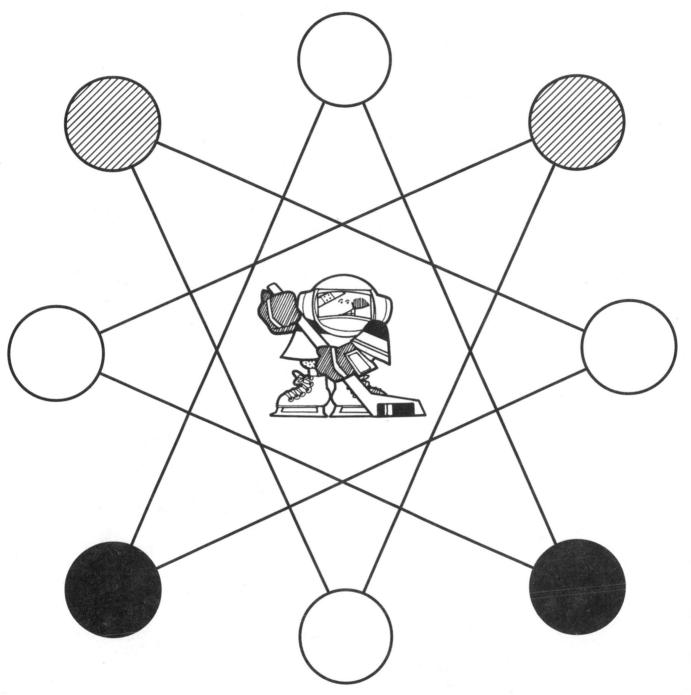

How many moves?

Game 1	Game 2	Game 3	Game 4	Game 5	Game 6

MAZITION
MAZE ADDITION

Skills
Addition, mental math

Materials Needed
- *Mazition* gameboard
- Scratch paper and pencil or calculator (optional)
- Markers

Object of Game
To find a path of numbers that adds up to a specific sum

Number of Players
One

Find the sums 37, 49, 61, 33 and 71 in this math maze.

START	5	12	11	3	END
	8	4	15	6	
	13	10	1	14	
	2	7	16	9	

How to Play

1. You are on a trip from the START side of the maze to the END side. During your trip you can only move to the right, up or down. (You cannot move left or diagonally.)

2. Begin on the START side of the number maze.

3. Add the numbers on a path (moving right, up or down) through the squares until you reach the END side of the maze and one of these sums:

37   49   61   33   71

Remember, you must begin on the START side and stop on the END side.

> **Hint:** You can use more than one number on the end side.

4. Place markers on your path as you go.

5. Write number equation path for each sum.

6. Find all five paths.

On Your Own
Create your own path to a sum. Write down the path. Ask a classmate to solve your Mazition.

MAZITION

Maze Addition

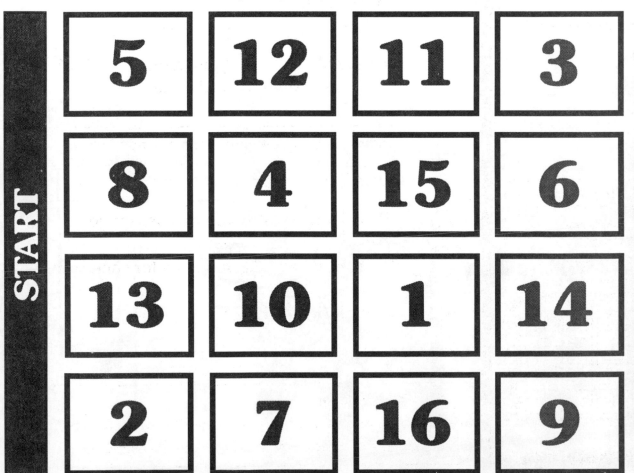

Find the sums 37, 49, 61, 33 and 71 in this math maze.

START

END

5	12	11	3
8	4	15	6
13	10	1	14
2	7	16	9

PENTOMINOES

Skills
Spatial relationships, problem solving

Materials Needed
- *Pentominoes* gameboard
- 12 pentomino pieces (page 100)

Object of Game
To fit all 12 pentomino pieces onto the gameboard

Number of Players
One

How to Play

1. Put pentomino pieces on the table and mix them up.

2. Place each piece on the gameboard grid so that all twelve pieces fill the board.

3. There is more than one way to complete this game. Once you have fit all the pieces on the gameboard, mix them up and try again.

PENTOMINOES

PICK 6

Skills
Problem solving, logic

Materials Needed
- *Pick 6* gameboard
- 6 markers (beans, coins, plastic chips)
- Stopwatch or clock with second hand (optional)

Object of Game
To place six markers on the board so that no two markers are in the same row, column or diagonal

Number of Players
One

How to Play

1. Place a marker in each square so there is only one in each row, column or diagonal.

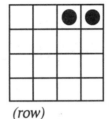

(row)

This isn't correct. These two markers are in the same row.

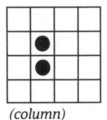

(column)

This isn't correct. These two markers are in the same column.

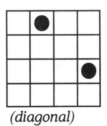

(diagonal)

This isn't correct. There are two markers in a diagonal.

2. Be patient. It may take you a while to find the answer.

Take the Pick 6 Challenge
Use a stopwatch or a clock to time yourself.
How fast did you complete the puzzle?

Instant Math Games That Teach   Creative Teaching Press

FREEDOM

Skill
Visual perception

Materials Needed
- *Freedom* gameboard
- Crayons (colored pencils, markers)

Object of Game
To determine which ring (A, B, C or D) could be cut to free all the rings

Number of Players
One

How to Play

1. Look at the four rings (A, B, C, D) very carefully.

2. Pretend that you have a pair of scissors and can cut only one ring to free the other three.

3. Study the picture to figure out which one you should cut.

4. If you need more help, color each ring a different color.

5. Can you think of something else to do that might help you?

Teacher Tip
You may want to reproduce a gameboard for each student.

HIDE AND SEEK

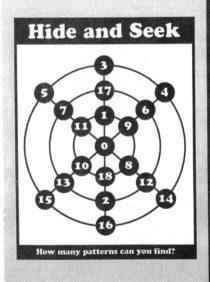

How to Play

1. A pattern is something that happens more than once. There are many patterns hidden on this gameboard—addition patterns. It is your job to discover as many of them as you can.

> **Hint:** The sum "19" is part of several hidden addition patterns on this gameboard. Can you find some?
>
> **Hint:** Follow the straight and the curved lines to find the hidden number addition patterns.

2. Write each addition pattern you find on a separate sheet of paper.

> **For example:** $3 + 16 = 19$
> $5 + 14 = 19$
> $15 + 4 = 19$

3. How many different addition patterns did you find?

Hide and Seek

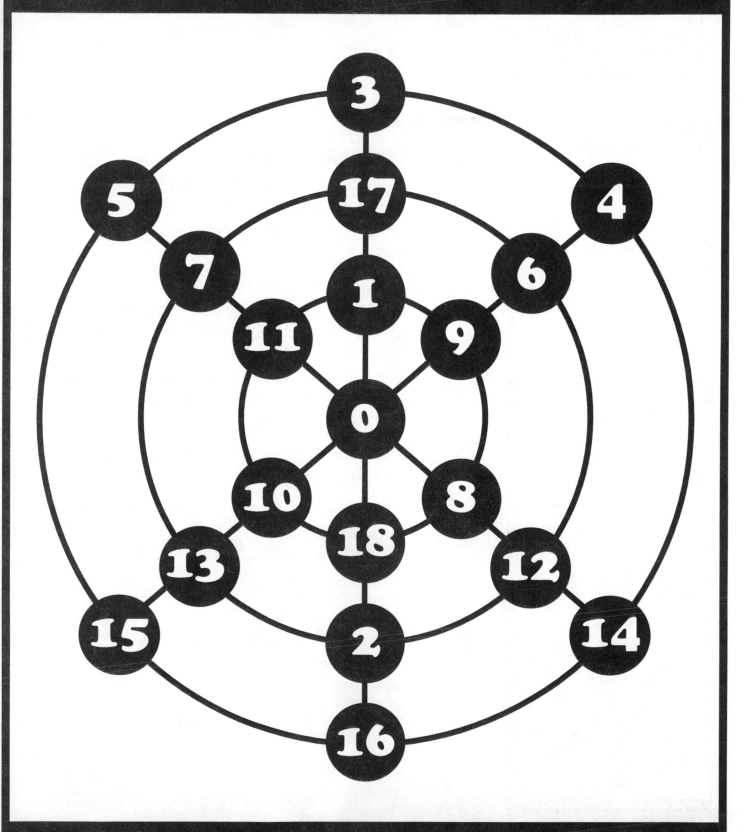

How many patterns can you find?

MIXED-UP MUSIC

Skills
Problem solving, logic

Materials Needed
- *Mixed-up Music* gameboard
- Number circles 1 through 8 (page 93)

Object of Game
To place each of the number circles inside the CD (compact disc) circles so that no two CDs connected by lines hold consecutive numbers

Number of Players
One

How to Play

1. Spread number circles on the table.

2. Place a number circle on each CD circle.

> **Hint:** Remember, any two numbers connected by a line cannot be consecutive.
>
> **For example:**
> - 1—2—3 are consecutive numbers.
> Their circles CANNOT be connected by lines.
> - 1—3—6 are not consecutive numbers.
> These CAN be connected by lines.

3. Once you've completed the puzzle, mix up the numbers and try again.

MIXED-UP MUSIC

DETOUR

DETOUR

Skill
Problem solving

Materials Needed
- *Detour* gameboard
- Pencil (crayon, marker)

Object of Game
To pass through all the circles with one continuous line

Number of Players
One

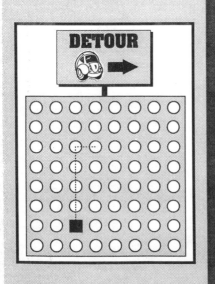

The Game
You're stuck in the city and must get out! Create your own detour by driving your pencil through the streets of Circle City. How quickly can you get out of the city? (You're out of the city when you've driven through each circle once and only once.)

How to Play

1. Place your pencil in the black square and begin following the dotted path.

2. Continue drawing a path through the remaining 58 circles, remembering that you can pass through each circle one time only.

3. You may not go off any path.

4. Once you've complete your journey, start again. There may be more than one way to get out of the city.

Teacher Tip
Laminate this gameboard and use with dry-erase pens or crayons or reproduce multiple copies for each player.

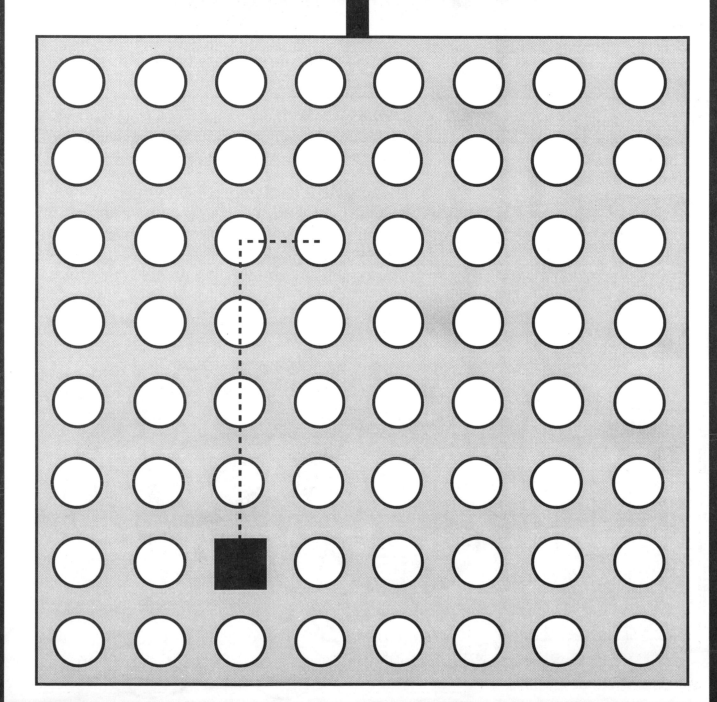

Instant Math Games That Teach

NEIGHBORS

Skills
Logic, problem solving

Materials Needed
- *Neighbors* gameboard
- Number squares 1 through 8 (page 94)

Object of Game
To place numbers on the gameboard so that no two consecutive numbers touch vertically, horizontally or diagonally

Number of Players
One

How to Play

1. Place one number in each square. Remember, no number can touch (either vertically, horizontally or diagonally) the number that comes before or after it.

> **For example:** The 2 cannot touch either the 1 or the 3 vertically, horizontally or diagonally.

2. This puzzle is challenging. Don't get discouraged if it takes you a while to find the solution.

PLANET PUZZLER

Skill
Addition, problem solving

Materials Needed
- *Planet Puzzler* gameboard
- Number circles 1 through 9 (page 93)

Object of Game
To place numbers on the planets and sun so every three in a row adds up to 15

Number of Players
One

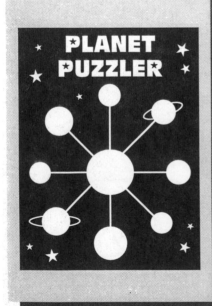

How to Play

Place the number circles on the planets and the sun so that every line of three numbers adds up to 15.

PLANET PUZZLER

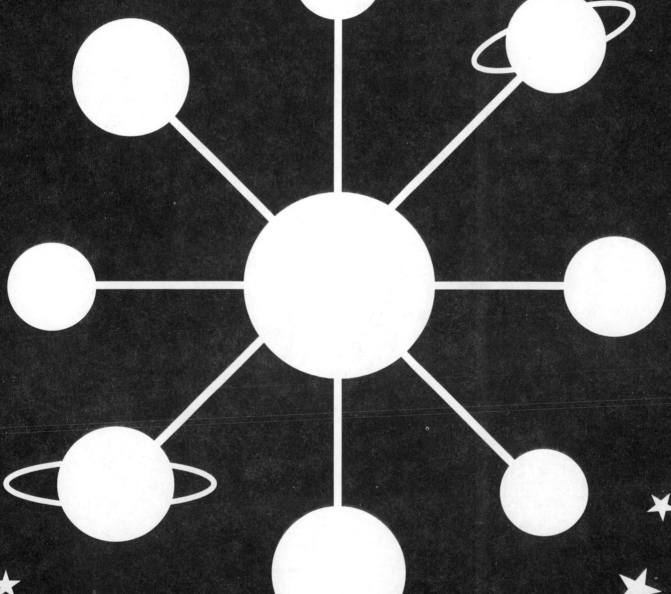

MARTIAN MATH

How to Play

1. Use the number tiles to help you figure out what numbers the Martian Math symbols represent.

> **Hint:**
> Start with the answer to the last problem: ✖▲

2. Write the Martian Math symbol for each number from 0 to 9 at the bottom of the gameboard.

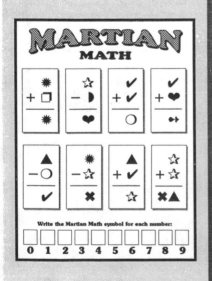

MARTIAN MATH

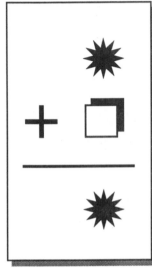

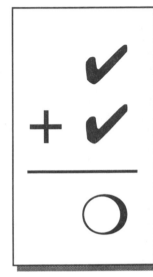

Write the Martian Math symbol for each number:

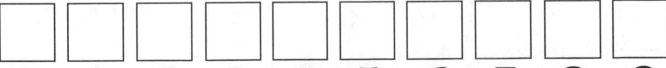

0 1 2 3 4 5 6 7 8 9

MAGIC 18

Skills
Addition, logic, problem solving

Materials Needed
- *Magic 18* gameboard
- Number circles 1 through 8 (page 93)

Object of Game
To place number circles so that each side of the diamond add up to 18

Number of Players
One

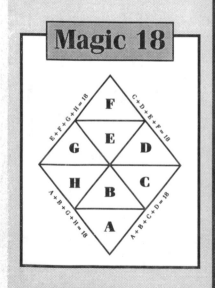

How to Play

1. Place one number in each circle on the gameboard.

2. You have correctly completed the *Magic 18* puzzle when the number circles in these triangles add up to 18:

$$A + B + C + D = 18$$

$$C + D + E + F = 18$$

$$E + F + G + H = 18$$

$$A + B + G + H = 18$$

Magic 18

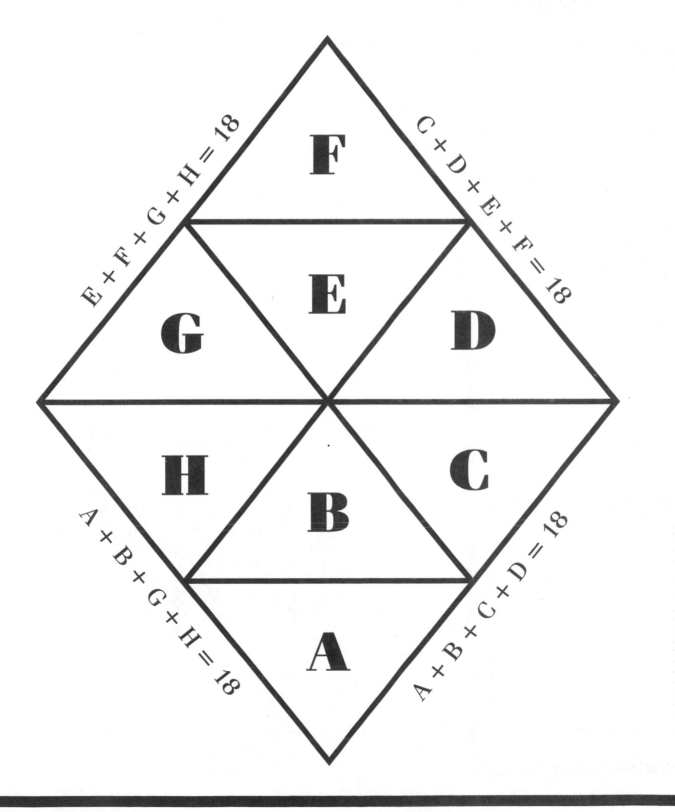

MYSTERIOUS WONDER WHEEL

Skills
Addition, problem solving

Materials Needed
- *Mysterious Wonder Wheel* gameboard
- Number circles 0 through 8 (page 93)

Object of Game
To place numbers on the Wonder Wheel so every three in a row adds up to 12

Number of Players
One

How to Play

Place the number circles on the Wonder Wheel squares and center circle so that every line of three numbers adds up to 12.

Take the Wonder Wheel Challenge
Use a stopwatch or a clock to time yourself. How fast did it take you solve the puzzle?

MYSTERIOUS WONDER WHEEL

Instant Math Games That Teach

Instant Math Games That Teach

Games for Two

SNAP

Skills
Strategy

Materials Needed
- *Snap* gameboard
- 21 markers (beans, small macaroni shells)

Object of Game
To force the other player to remove the last marker

Number of Players
Two

How to Play

1. Place all 21 markers inside the alligator's mouth.

2. Each player takes turns removing one or two beans from the mouth.

3. The person who forces the other player to remove the last bean is the winner.

Super Snap Variation
Using 50 markers, each player removes one to six at a time.

KABOOM!

Skills
Strategy

Materials Needed
- *Kaboom!* gameboard
- 9 markers (beans, coins, plastic chips)
- Scrap paper and pencil

Object of Game
To force the other player to take the last marker

Number of Players
Two

How to Play

1. Put a marker on each square on the gameboard.

2. The first player can remove one or more markers, but only from one row.

3. Players take turns removing markers, until only one marker is left on the board. The player who takes the last marker on the gameboard loses and must say, "Kaboom!"

4. Record winner on scratch paper.

5. Play at least 10 games. Who won the most games?

Instant Math Games That Teach

TRIPLE PLAY

41	20	40	23	46	18
43	38	19	44	40	21
18	42	36	39	22	41
37	21	20	41	42	23
45	19	40	22	43	40

How to Play

1. The first player rolls the dice.

2. The player may put a marker on the two numbers rolled or on their sum.

> **For example:** If a player rolls a 20 and an 18, a marker can be placed on any 20 and 18 or on their sum, 38.

3. The next player rolls the dice and places a marker on each of the numbers rolled or their sum, but only if the numbers aren't already covered. There can only be one marker per space.

4. If a player cannot cover a space, he or she loses a turn.

5. The first player with three of his or her markers in a horizontal, vertical or diagonal line is the winner!

41	20	40	23	46	18
43	38	19	44	40	21
18	42	36	39	22	41
37	21	20	41	42	23
45	19	40	22	43	40

SINK OR SWIM

Skills
Addition, subtraction, multiplication, recognizing odd and even numbers, mental math

Materials Needed
- *Sink or Swim* gameboard
- 1 marker for each player
- 1 pair of dice (page 97)
- Calculator (optional)

Object of Game
To reach one of the ends

Number of Players
Two

The Game
Two divers are diving for buried treasure. Their tanks begin to run low on air. See which diver is the first to either sink and be eaten or swim and be rescued.

How to Play:

1. Each player puts his/her marker on a START circle.

2. Player A rolls the dice and either adds, subtracts or multiplies the two numbers.

3. If the answer is an odd number, the player moves one space toward the shark.

4. If the answer is an even number, the player moves one space toward the life raft.

5. Player B takes his/her turn.

6. Players alternate turns until one player reaches either the life raft or the shark. Then points are scored:
- A player reaching the life raft first earns 5 points.
- A player reaching the shark first earns 3 points.

7. Play as many games as you can in 10 minutes. The player with the greatest number of points is the winner.

SINK OR SWIM

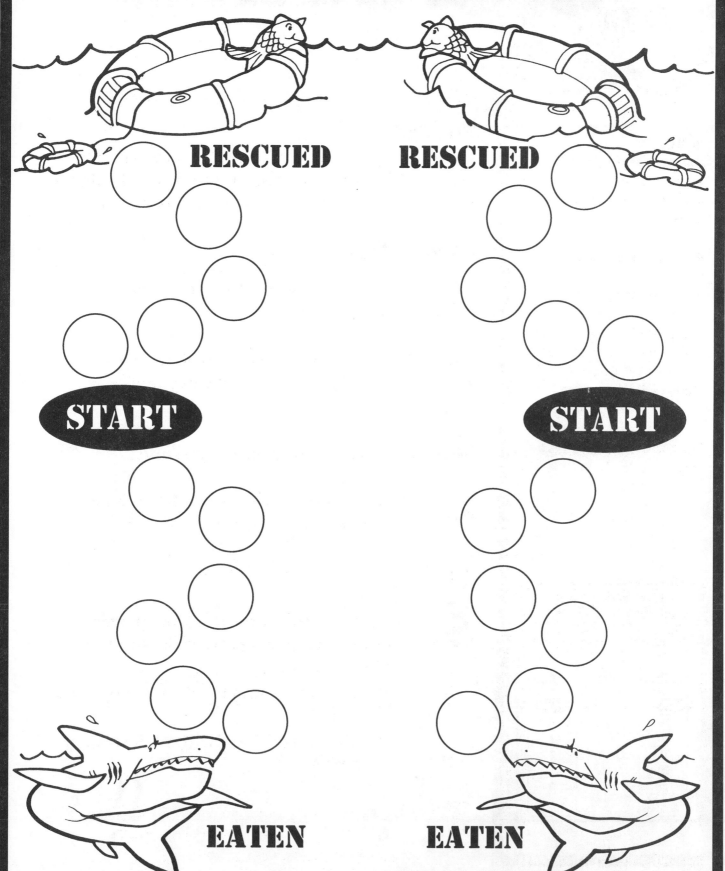

RESCUED   RESCUED

START   START

EATEN   EATEN

LIGHTNING

Skills
Place value, mental addition

Materials Needed
- *Lightning* gameboard
- 2 markers for each player
- Pair of dice with numbers 1 to 6 printed on sides (page 97)

Object of Game
To be the first player to reach 100

Number of Players
Two

How to Play

1. Each player places one marker at the bottom of each column.

2. Player A rolls the dice and adds up the numbers. Player A moves his/her marker to the correct space in the ones' column. If the sum is beyond nine, the player begins using the marker in the tens' column.

> **For example:** 12 would be 10 and 2.

3. Player B rolls the dice, adds up the numbers and moves.

4. Players alternate turns, rolling the dice, adding the sum to their previous score and moving their markers.

5. The first player to move quickly (like LIGHTNING) and reach 100 is the winner!

THREE-IN-A-ROW

THREE
IN-A-ROW

Skills
Strategy

Materials Needed
- *Three-in-a-Row* gameboard
- 2 sets of 3 markers (for example: 3 pennies and 3 nickels)
- Scratch paper and pencil

Object of Game
To place three markers in a row

Number of Players
Two

How to Play

1. Players alternate turns placing one marker at a time in the empty circles on the gameboard until they have no markers left.

2. Then Player #1 moves one of his markers one space along a line to an empty circle. The player may not jump over any markers.

3. The game continues with players alternating turns until one player gets all three of his/her markers in a row, either across, up and down, or diagonally.

4. Players should have a 5- or 10-game tournament. Keep track of wins to decide who is the tournament champ.

IN-A-ROW

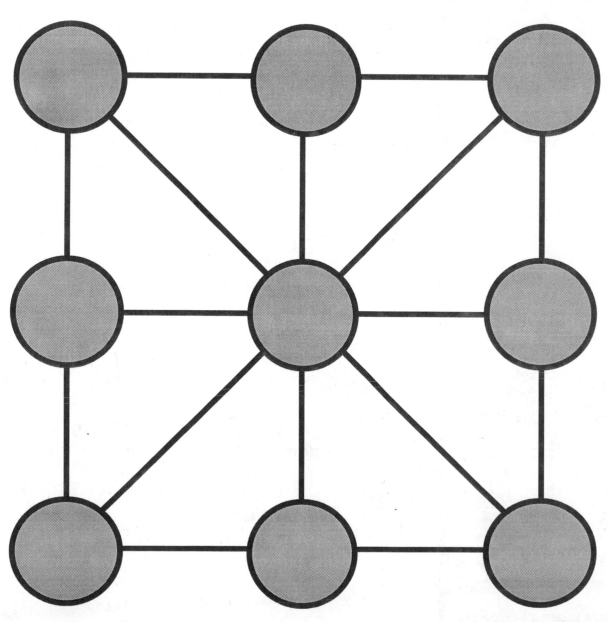

ADD IT UP

Skills
Mental addition, strategy

Materials Needed
- *Add It Up* gameboard
- *Add It Up* spinner
  (page 96)
- 2 sets of 9 markers
  (for example, 9 pennies
  and 9 beans)

Object of Game
To attain the lowest score

Number of Players
Two

How to Play

1. Player A spins the spinner and has the option of either covering that number on his/her column or covering any numbers that when added together equal that number.

> **For example:** If a player spins a 7, he/she has the option of covering the 7 or any combination of 7 such as 5 and 2, 4 and 3, 6 and 1, or 4, 2 and 1.

2. Player B spins and covers the number or numbers in his/her column.

3. Players alternate spins until each player can no longer cover numbers on his/her column.

4. Each player adds up the uncovered numbers in his/her column.

5. The player with the lowest score is the winner.

6. Players should have a 5- or 10-game tournament. Keep track of wins to decide who is the Add It Up champ.

Instant Math Games That Teach   Creative Teaching Press

ADD IT UP

Player A

9
8
7
6
5
4
3
2
1

Player B

9
8
7
6
5
4
3
2
1

COVER UP
GREATER, LESS, EQUAL

Skills
Determining numbers that are greater than, less than, equal to; problem solving

Materials Needed
- *Cover Up* gameboard
- *Cover Up* spinner (page 96)
- 1 number die with the numbers 1 to 6 on its sides (page 97)
- 2 sets of 13 markers

Object of Game
To be the first player to place five markers in a row, column or diagonal

Number of Players
Two

How to Play

1. Player A rolls the die and then spins the spinner. Using one of his/her markers, the player "covers up" any number on the board that matches.

> **For example:** If a player rolls a "3" and spins the "less than" sign (<), the player can cover either the 1 or 2.
>
> If a player rolls a "6" and spins the "greater than" sign (>), the player can cover any number higher than a 6.
>
> If a player rolls a "5" and an "equal" sign (=), the player can only cover the 5.

2. Player B rolls the die, spins the spinner and "covers up" a matching number.

3. If a number has already been covered, the player must either make another choice (if possible) or skip his/her turn.

4. The first player to cover up a row, column or diagonal is the winner.

GREATER, LESS, EQUAL

1	2	3	4	5
6	7	8	9	10
11	12	13	14	15
16	17	18	19	20
21	22	23	24	25

EXACT CHANGE

Skills
Mental addition, strategy

Materials Needed
- *Exact Change* gameboard
- 2 sets of 8 markers (for example, 8 beans and 8 plastic chips)
- Scratch paper and pencil (optional)

Object of Game
To choose numbers whose sum equals exactly $1.00

Number of Players
Two

How to Play

1. Players take turns putting one marker on any uncovered number.

2. Each time a marker is placed on the board, that number is added to the sum of the player's previous marker(s).

3. Keep your eyes open. You will need to use strategy to keep the other player from making $1.00.

4. The winner is the first player to make exactly $1.00.

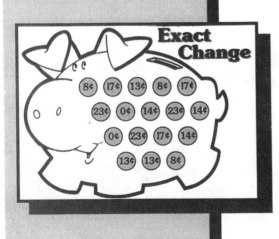

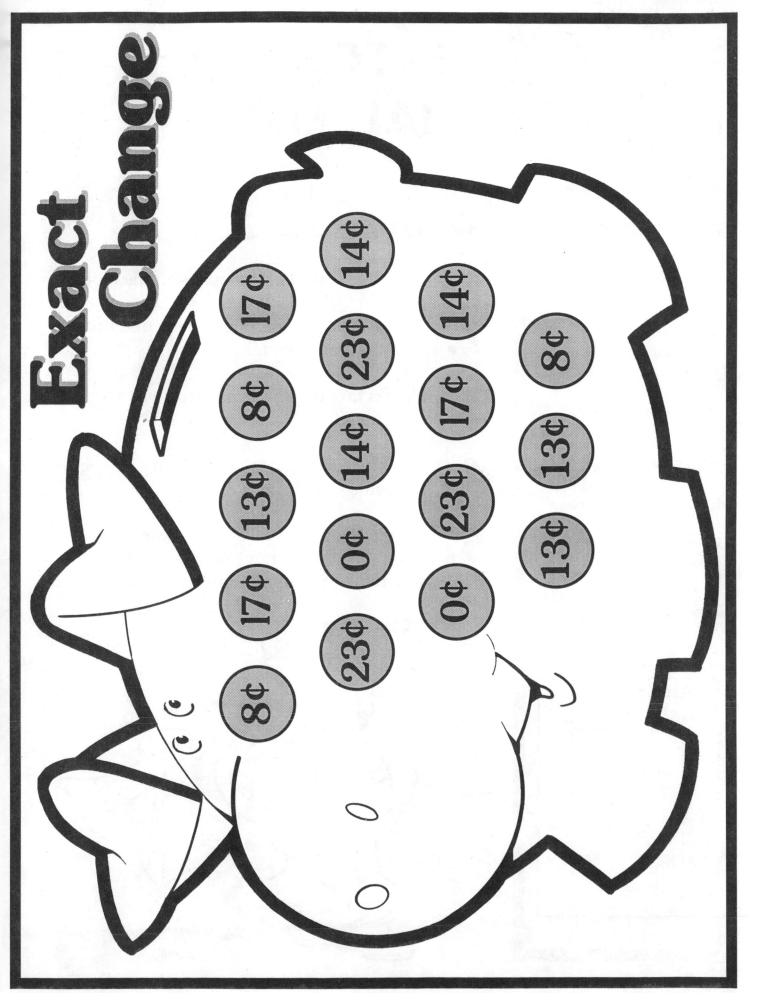

Exact Change

PENTOMINO CHALLENGE

Skills
Spatial relationships, strategy

Materials Needed
- *Pentomino Challenge* gameboard
- 12-piece pentomino set (page 100)
- Scratch paper and pencil

Object of Game
To be the last player to place a pentomino piece

Number of Players
Two

How to Play

1. Place the 12 pentomino pieces on the table.

2. The first player chooses one piece and fits it on the gameboard.

3. Players take turns placing pieces on the gameboard.

4. The last player who is able to fit a piece onto the gameboard is the winner.

5. Players should have a 5- or 10-game tournament. Keep track of wins to decide who is the Pentomino Challenge champ.

Pentomino Challenge

ROUND UP

Skill
Strategy

Materials Needed
- *Round Up* gameboard
- 2 sets of 4 markers (for example: 4 pennies and 4 nickels)

Object of Game
To line up three of your markers horizontally, vertically or diagonally

Number of Players
Two

How to Play

1. Player A puts his/her markers on the star boxes.

2. Player B puts his/her markers on the circle boxes.

3. Player A moves one of his/her markers one space to the right, to the left, up or down but NOT DIAGONALLY.

4. Player B moves one of his/her markers.

5. Players alternate moves, moving their markers to empty boxes.

> **Important:** A player may not jump over a marker or take a marker off the gameboard. If a square is occupied, no other marker can be moved into that space.

6. A player wins when he/she lines up three markers either horizontally, vertically or diagonally.

Instant Math Games That Teach

TIC TAC 15

Skills
Addition, strategy

Materials Needed
- *Tic Tac 15* gameboard
- *Tic Tac 15* game cards (from bottom of gameboard)
- Scratch paper and pencil

Object of Game
To line up three numbers whose sum equals 15 either horizontally, vertically or diagonally

Number of Players
Two

How to Play

1. Cut out the nine numbers at the bottom of the gameboard and place them face down on the table.

2. Each player alternates picking a card and placing it in any square.

3. Players continue placing cards until the sum of three numbers in a vertical, horizontal or diagonal row equals 15. The player who puts down the winning card says, "Tic Tac 15." If no players reach 15, a new game is begun.

4. Players should have a 5- or 10-game tournament. Keep track of wins to decide who is the Tic Tac 15 champ.

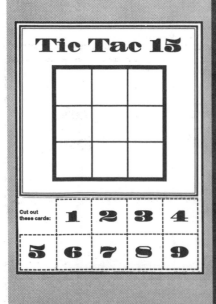

Tic Tac 15

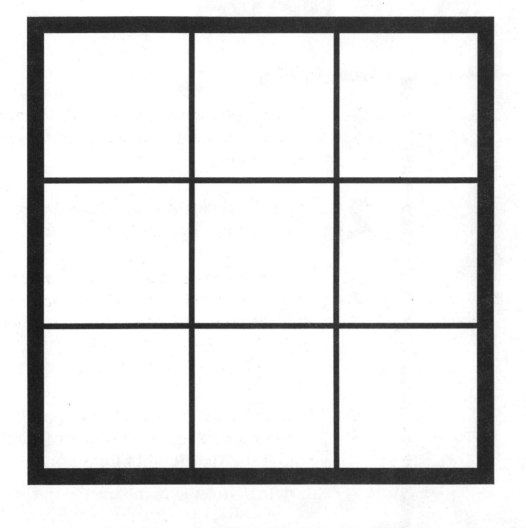

Cut out these cards:

1 2 3 4

5 6 7 8 9

• AH-HA
• POWER
• NADA

Skill
Logic

Materials Needed
- *Ah-ha* • *Power* • *Nada* gameboard
- Scratch paper and pencil

Object of Game
To identify a number in as few guesses as possible

Number of Players
Two

• AH-HA
• POWER
• NADA

	Guess	Ah-ha Correct digit, Wrong position	Power Correct digit, Correct position	Nada Nothing correct
1				
2				
3				
4				
5				
6				
7				
8				
9				
10				
11				
12				
13				
14				
15				

How to Play

1. The first player thinks of a two-digit number, writes it on a paper and turns it face down on the table.

2. The second player, the guesser, writes his/her guess on line #1 on the gameboard.

3. The first player writes an X in the correct clue column of line one. Here are the clue guidelines:

- The **Ah-ha** clue means the guesser has one correct digit, but in the wrong position.

- The **Power** clue means the guesser has one correct digit in the correct position.

- The **Nada** clue means the guesser has nothing correct.

4. The second player continues guessing numbers, using the clues to help.

5. The game is over when the correct number is guessed.

6. More games can be played using copies of the gameboard or scratch paper. Players should switch roles each game.

- # AH-HA
- # POWER
- # NADA

	Guess	Ah-ha Correct digit, Wrong position	Power Correct digit, Correct position	Nada Nothing correct
1				
2				
3				
4				
5				
6				
7				
8				
9				
10				
11				
12				
13				
14				
15				

Instant Math Games That Teach

Creative Teaching Press

Games for Two or More

SNAIL'S PACE

How to Play

1. Both players place their markers on the
START box in the middle of the snail.

2. The first player rolls the dice and moves
his/her marker according to this chart:

> **Move 1** space if two even numbers come up.
>
> **Move 2** spaces if two odd numbers come up.
>
> **Move 3** spaces if one even and one odd number
> come up.

3. Players alternate turns.

4. When a player lands on a special square,
the directions must be followed.

5. The first player to reach the finish line
is the winner.

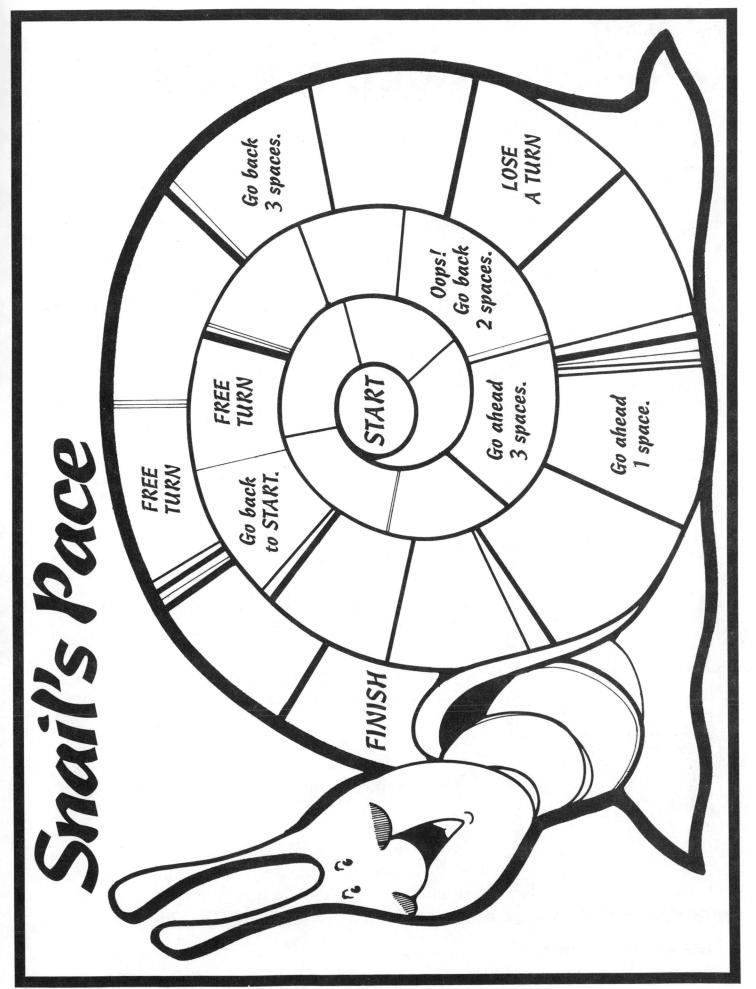

Snail's Pace

Go back 3 spaces.

LOSE A TURN

Oops! Go back 2 spaces.

FREE TURN

FREE TURN

START

Go ahead 3 spaces.

Go ahead 1 space.

Go back to START.

FINISH

SPILL THE BEANS

Skills
Addition, subtraction, multiplication, mental math

Materials Needed
- *Spill the Beans* gameboard
- 1 cup
- 2 beans
- Scratch paper and pencil

Object of Game
To be the first player to reach zero

Number of Players
Two or more

Spill the Beans

5	3	2	4
6	4	0	1
2	3	1	8
0	2	3	4
9	1	4	7

How to Play

1. Put the two beans in a cup.

2. The first player spills the beans onto the gameboard.

3. The player either adds or multiplies (teacher's choice) the numbers the beans landed on. If a bean lands on a line, it can be thrown again.

4. Using scratch paper (if necessary), the player subtracts the answer from 50.

> **For example:** The player spills the beans onto a 2 and a 5. If multiplying, the player says the product, 10, and then subtracts that number from 50.
>
> 50 – 10 = 40.

5. After each player spills the beans, his or her answer is subtracted from their last number on the score sheet.

6. Players take turns spilling the beans and subtracting until one player reaches zero.

> ## Variations on Spill the Beans
> Play 100-point *Spill the Beans*. Begin the game by subtracting from 100. Or how about a 3-bean game? Throw 3 beans and add the numbers together, then subtract from 100.

Spill the Beans

5	3	2	4
6	4	0	1
2	3	1	8
0	2	3	4
9	1	4	7

BLANK CHECK

Skills
Reading money amounts, place value, strategy

Materials Needed
- 1 *Blank Check* gameboard for each player
- *Blank Check* spinner (page 96)
- Pencil

Object of Game
To write the largest amount on each check

Number of Players
Two or more

How to Play

Check #1

1. The players alternate spinning the spinner for three times total. After each spin, each player writes that number in any of the three lines on his/her blank check.

2. After the third spin, the players read their check amounts aloud. The player with the biggest check wins. The winner puts a check mark by his/her winning amount.

Checks #2 through #8

3. Play continues for checks 2 through 8 with players alternating spinning. In each round, the spinner is spun as many times as there are blank lines on the check.

4. When all eight checks have been written, each player counts up the number of winning checks on his/her gameboard. The player with the most check marks is the Blank Check champion.

Teeny Tiny Checks
Try this. Instead of trying to write the biggest check you can, try writing the smallest check. The game is played as before, except the player with the check written for the least amount of money wins.

Instant Math Games That Teach Creative Teaching Press

Blank Check

Check #1

$ __ . __ __

Check #2

$ __ . __ __

Check #3

$ __ __ . __ __

Check #4

$ __ __ . __ __

Check #5

$ __ __ __ . __ __

Check #6

$ __ __ __ . __ __

Check #7

$ __ , __ __ __ . __ __

Check #8

$ __ __ , __ __ __ . __ __

CONTINENT HOP

Skill
Multiplication facts

Materials Needed
- *Continent Hop* gameboard
- *Continent Hop* spinner with numbers 1 through 9 (page 96)
- Scratch paper and pencil
- 1 marker for each player

Object of Game
To be the first player to reach North America

Number of Players
Two or more

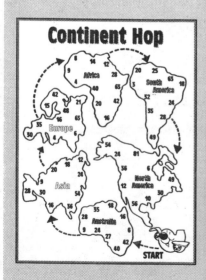

The Game
Each player is a world traveler, starting an around-the-world journey in a supersonic jet. By spinning two numbers and multiplying them together, a traveler can move from continent to continent. Each player's final destination is North America.

How to Play

1. The first player spins the spinner twice, writing the numbers on scratch paper.

2. The player multiplies the two numbers, saying the product aloud.

3. If the product is found on the first continent, Australia, the player moves his/her marker there. If the product is not on the Australian continent or if the player gives the wrong product, his/her marker cannot move.

4. All players must follow the arrows, moving from one continent to another. No continents can be skipped.

5. Players take turns spinning, giving the product and moving (when possible).

6. The first player to reach North America is the winner.

Continent Hop

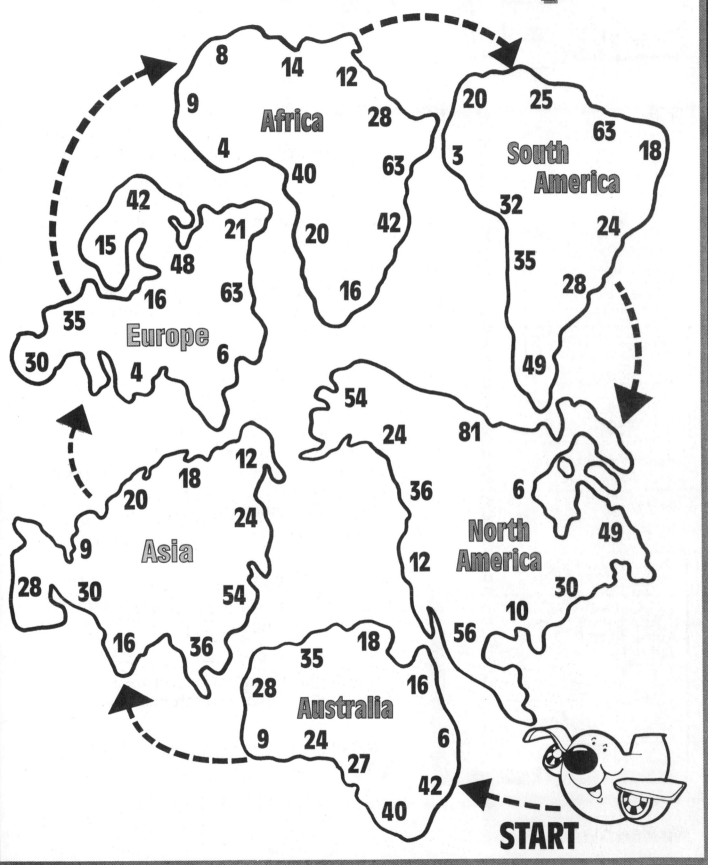

CROSS THE RIVER

Skills
Spatial relationships, geometric relationships

Materials Needed
- *Cross the River* gameboard
- *Cross the River* spinner (page 95)
- 1 set of tangrams for each player (page 99)
- 1 marker for each player

Object of Game
To be the first player to cross the river

Number of Players
Two or more

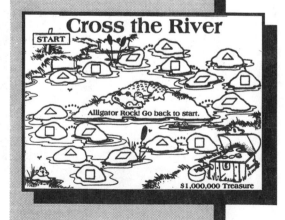

How to Play

1. Players place their markers on START.

2. The first player spins the spinner and moves his/her marker the number of stones shown on the spinner.

3. The number on the spinner also tells the player how many tangram pieces must be used to make the shape he or she has landed on.

> **For example:** If a player spins a "3" and lands on a triangle, the player must use exactly three tangram pieces to make a triangle.

4. If the player makes the shape, the player stays on the stone.

5. If the player cannot make the shape, he or she moves back that number of spaces.

> **Important:** More than one player can land on a stone at the same time.

6. Players take turns spinning, moving and creating tangram shapes. The first player to cross the river is the winner!

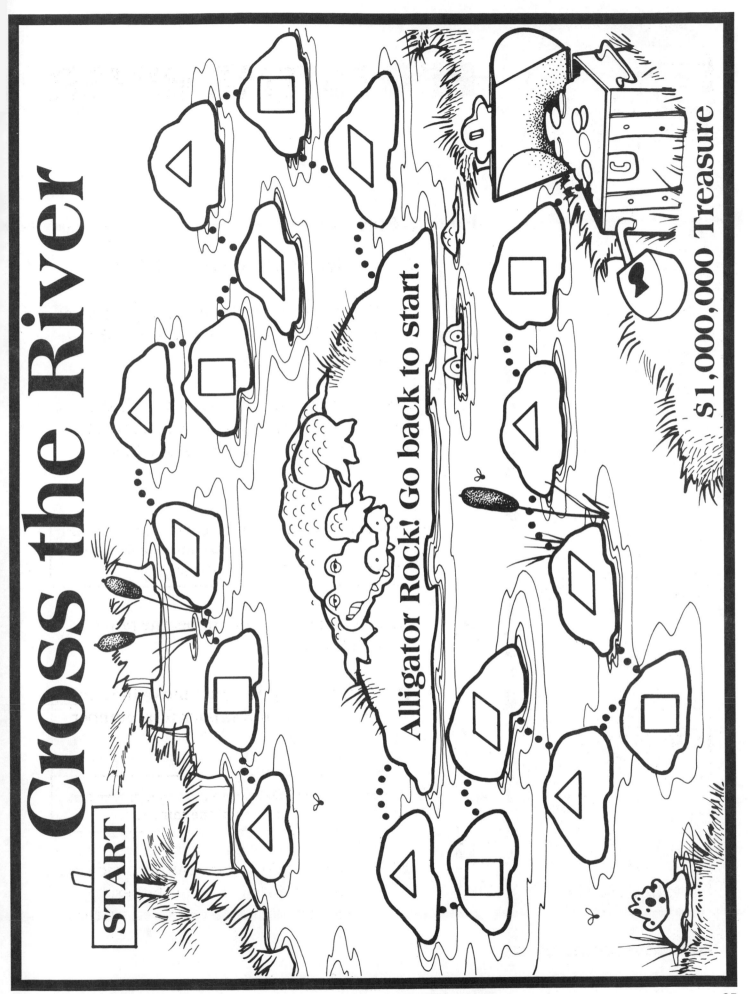

Cross the River

START

Alligator Rock! Go back to start.

$1,000,000 Treasure

BLACK HOLE

Skill
Subtraction

Materials Needed
- *Black Hole* gameboard
- 1 marker (coin or plastic chip)
- Scratch paper and pencil

Object of Game
To be the first player to reach 100 or less

Number of Players
Two or more

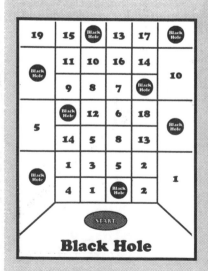

Black Hole

How to Play

1. Each player begins with 200 points.

2. The first player places the marker on START.

3. Using the eraser end of a pencil as a cue stick, the player shoots the marker toward the numbers.

4. The number the marker lands on is subtracted from that player's 200 points.

> **Important:** If the marker lands on a line between spaces, the player subtracts the larger number.

5. Players alternate turns, subtracting from their previous scores.

>
> **Watch Out!** When the marker lands in a Black Hole, the player cannot subtract anything from his/her score.

6. The first player to reach 100 is the winner.

19	15	Black Hole	13	17	Black Hole
Black Hole	11	10	16	14	10
	9	8	7	Black Hole	
5	Black Hole	12	6	18	Black Hole
	14	5	8	13	
Black Hole	1	3	5	2	1
	4	1	Black Hole	2	

START

Black Hole

MONSTER MATH

How to Play

1. Each player is given a gameboard and 2 markers.

2. The first player takes a handful of beans. Before counting the beans, each player estimates whether the handful is an odd or even number. Each player then places one marker in the odd or even box on his/her gameboard.

3. Each player also estimates how many beans will remain after the player holding the beans places them into groups of four. Each player places one marker in either the 0, 1, 2 or 3 box on his/her gameboard.

4. Now the player with the handful of beans begins placing four beans on each bat. Extras are placed in the remainder box.
- If 0 or 2 beans remain, the remainder is even.
- If 1 or 3 beans remain, the remainder is odd.

5. Each player scores points for estimating correctly. Each player receives:

4 points for correctly estimating odd or even.

2 points for correctly estimating the remainder.

Individual scores are kept on scratch paper.

6. Play alternates with each player taking a handful of beans, all players estimating odd/even and the remainder, and the player placing the beans on the bats.

7. The winner is the first player to score 50 points.

MONSTER MATH

Even	Odd
0	1
2	3

Remainder

Instant Math Games That Teach

Creative Teaching Press

Appendix and Game Answers

MARKERS

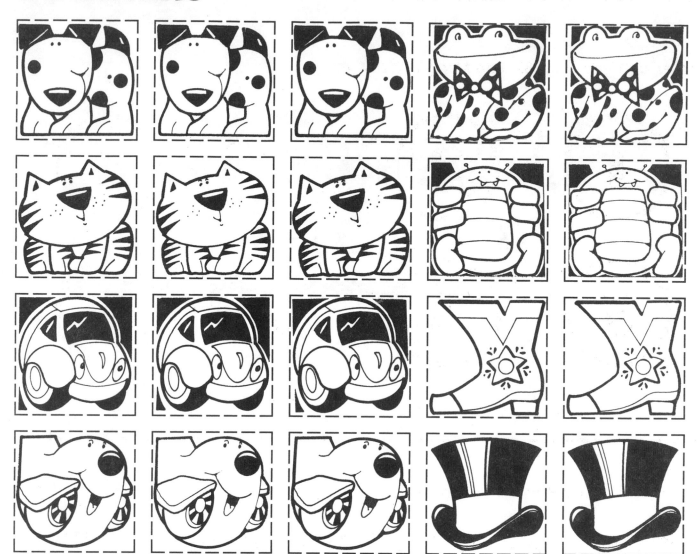

INDIVIDUAL COUNTERS

NUMBER CIRCLES

Mixed-up Music (page 32) and *Magic 18* (page 42)

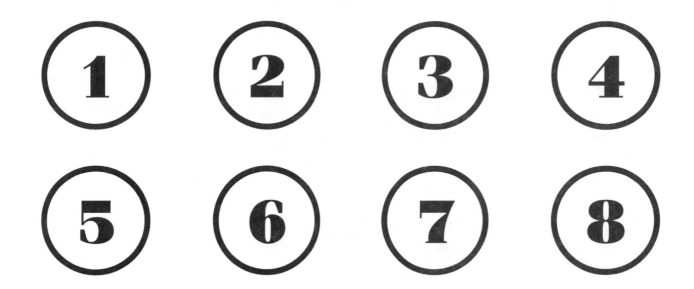

Use circles 1–9 for *Planet Puzzler* (page 38) and 0–8 for *Mysterious Wonder Wheel* (page 44).

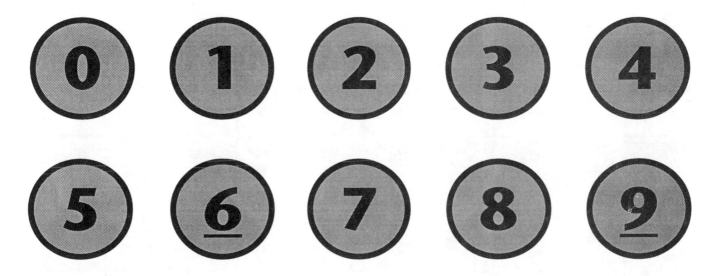

NUMBER SQUARES & TILES

Number Squares for *Neighbors* (page 36)

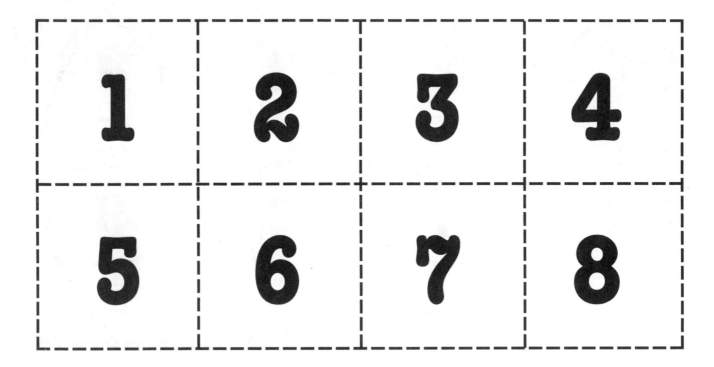

Number Tiles for *Martian Math* (page 40)

0	1	2	3	4	5	6	7	8	9
0	1	2	3	4	5	6	7	8	9
0	1	2	3	4	5	6	7	8	9
0	1	2	3	4	5	6	7	8	9
0	1	2	3	4	5	6	7	8	9

SPINNERS

This blank spinner can be used with any game requiring dice. Fill in numbers as described in game directions.

Cut out the spinner and arrow. Attach the arrow with a brad.

Option: Place the end of a paper clip over the dot on the spinner. Put a pencil point inside the paper clip on the dot. Hold the pencil firmly and spin the paper clip.

Spinner for *Cross the River* (page 84)

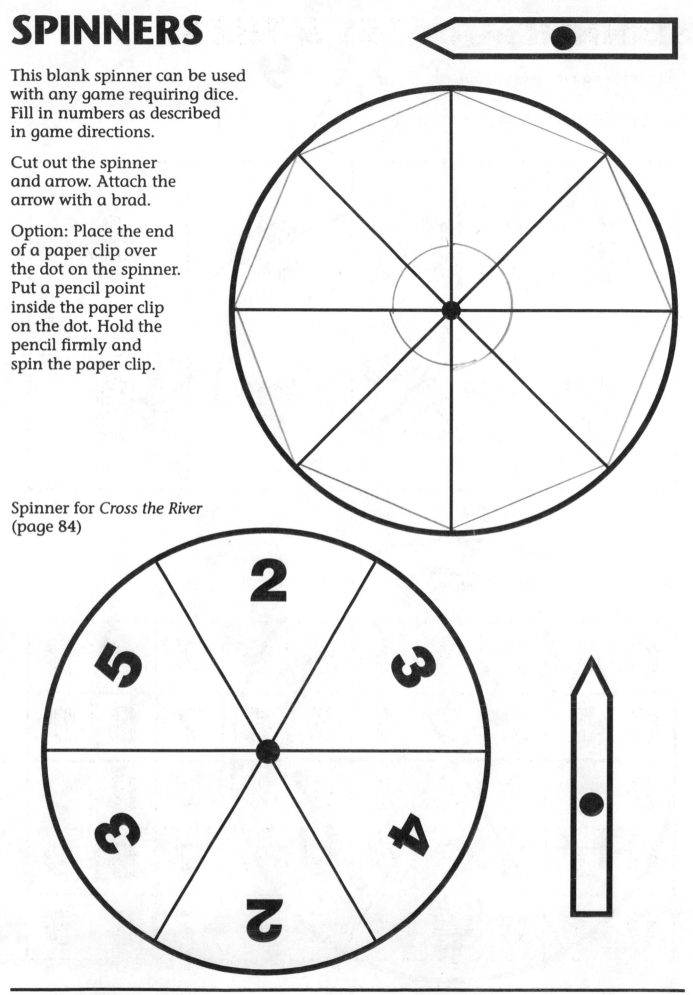

SPINNERS

Spinner for *Add It Up* (page 60),
Blank Check (page 80), and
Continent Hop (page 82)

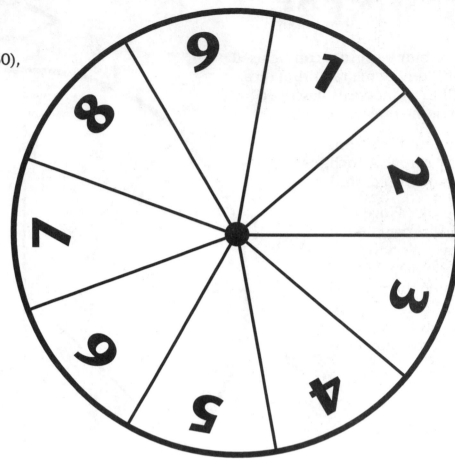

Spinner for *Cover Up* (page 62)

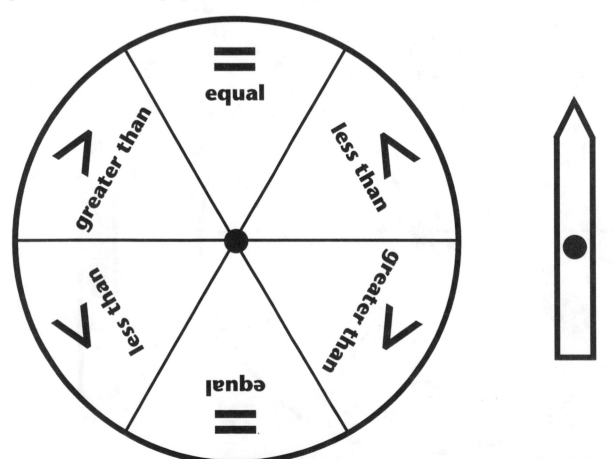

Instant Math Games That Teach

DICE

Reproduce for *Lightning* (page 56), *Cover Up* (page 62), and *Snail's Pace* (page 76).
Cut out, fold on dotted lines and glue together.

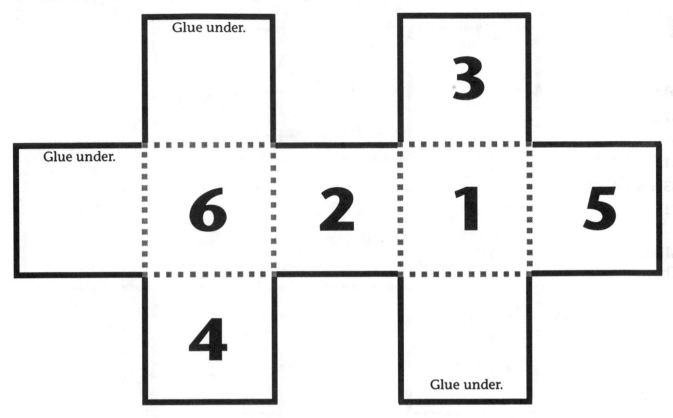

Reproduce for *Sink or Swim* (page 54).
Cut out, fold on dotted lines and glue together.

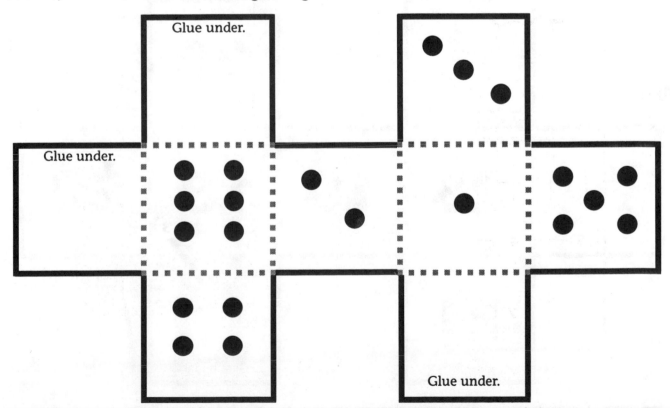

DICE

Reproduce for *Triple Play* (page 52).
Cut out, fold on dotted lines and glue together.

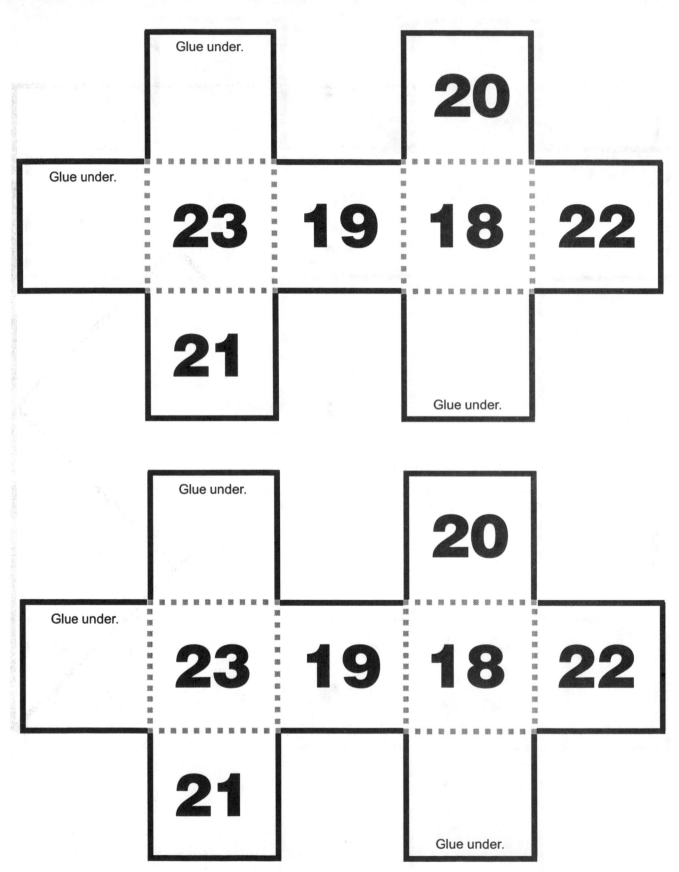

Instant Math Games That Teach Creative Teaching Press

TANGRAM PIECES

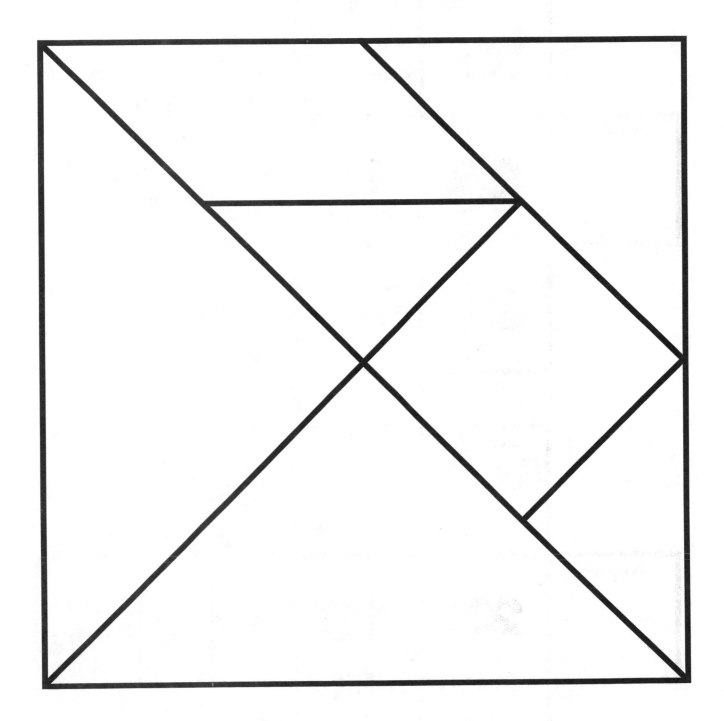

PENTOMINOES

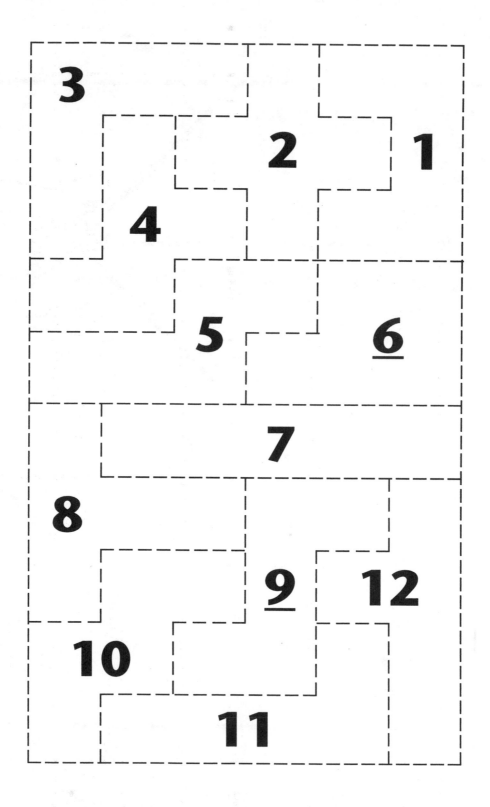

MATH WALLET

Make a Math Wallet for each game. On the outside of the wallet, write the name of the game and the number of game pieces inside.

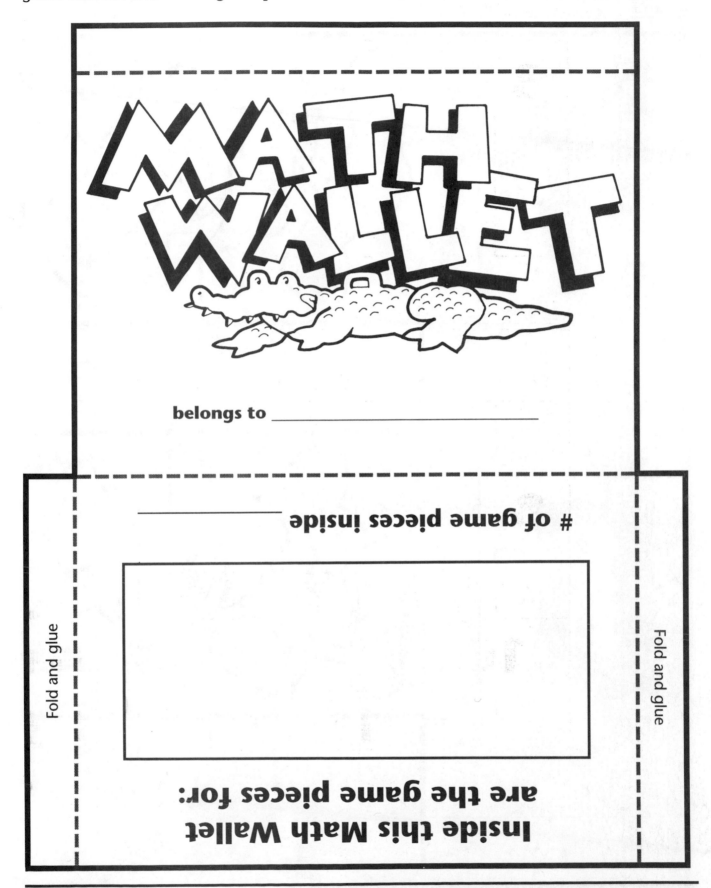

belongs to _____

# of game pieces inside _____

Fold and glue

Fold and glue

Inside this Math Wallet are the game pieces for:

Instant Math Games That Teach

MATH TROPHY

Write your name on the line and color. Then cut along the solid lines and fold on the dotted lines to form the base for the trophy. Staple or glue the trophy together where marked.

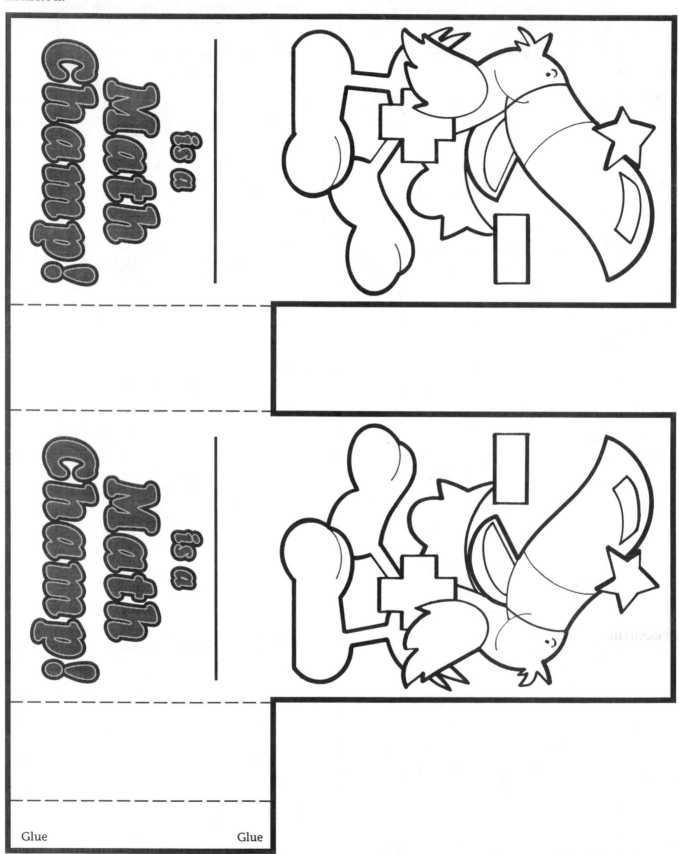

Instant Math Games That Teach   Creative Teaching Press

GAME ANSWERS

Add It Up (page 61)

1	15	8	12
10	6	20	4
3	16	2	13
8	5	14	7

Changing Places (page 17)

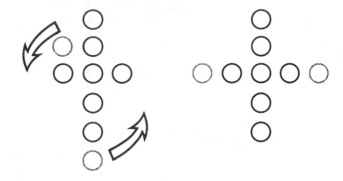

Detour (page 35)

There may be other solutions.

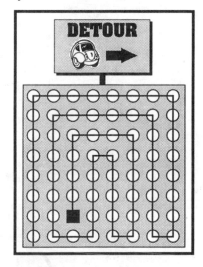

Freedom (page 29)

Cut circle C

Hide and Seek (page 31)

- The sum of the numbers in all 3 circles is 57.
- The sum of the numbers in all 3 diameters is 57.
- The sum of the numbers opposite one another on the same circle is 19.
- Look for more!

Finding 50 (page 19)

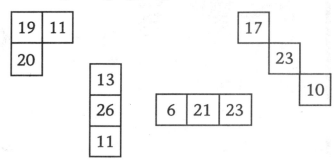

Magic 18 (page 43)

There may be other solutions.

Martian Math (page 41)

0	=	☐	4	=	◯	8	=	☆
1	=	✖	5	=	◗	9	=	✳
2	=	✔	6	=	▲			
3	=	❤	7	=	✚			

GAME ANSWERS (continued)

Mazition (Maze Addition) (page 23)

$37 = 5 + 12 + 11 + 3 + 6$

$49 = 13 + 10 + 1 + 16 + 9$

$61 = 8 + 4 + 15 + 11 + 3 + 6 + 14$

$33 = 8 + 4 + 15 + 6$

$71 = 13 + 10 + 4 + 12 + 11 + 15 + 6$

Mixed-up Music (page 33)

There may be other solutions.

Mysterious Wonder Wheel (page 45)

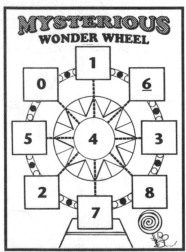

Neighbors (page 37)

There may be other solutions.

Pick 6 (page 27)

There may be other solutions.

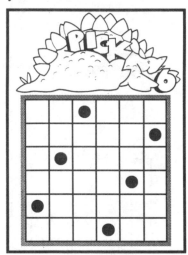

Planet Puzzler (page 39)